CLOUDS

TIM HARRIS

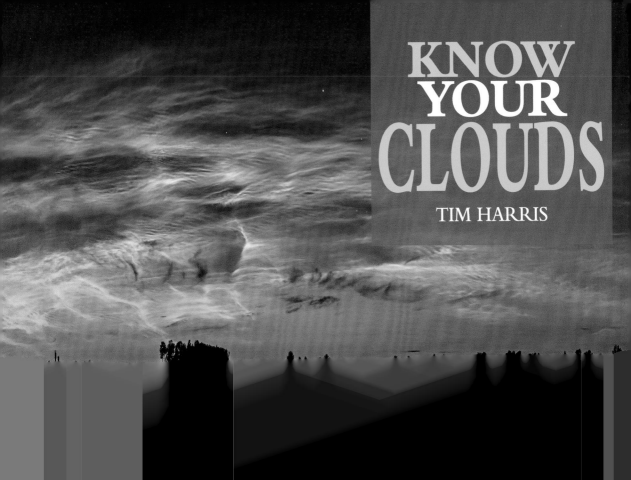

KNOW YOUR CLOUDS

TIM HARRIS

Know Your Clouds

Old Pond Publishing is an imprint of Fox Chapel Publishers International Ltd.

Project Team
Consultant Publisher: Helen Brocklehurst
Editor: Sue Viccars
Designer: Emily Kingston

ISBN 978-1-913618-09-4

A catalogue record for this book is available from the British Library.

Fox Chapel Publishing
903 Square Street
Mount Joy, PA 17552

Fox Chapel Publishers International Ltd.
3 The Bridle Way, Selsey, Chichester
West Sussex PO20 0RS, U.K.

www.oldpond.com

Printed and bound in China

10 9 8 7 6 5 4 3 2

Cover photo: Fair-weather cumulus on a summer afternoon
Photo on pages 2–3: Ominous yet benign, noctilucent clouds glow in the night sky over Lithuania

Contents

Foreword 7

The nature and naming
of clouds 9

How clouds form 11

Cumulus family **12**

1 Fair weather cumulus . . . 14

2 Medium cumulus 16

3 Towering cumulus 18

4 Fire cloud 20

5 Cumulonimbus 22

6 Anvil cloud 24

7 Mammatus 26

Stratus family **28**

8 Featureless stratus 30

9 Nimbostratus 32

Altocumulus family **34**

10 Mackerel sky 36

11 Lens and pancake clouds . 38

12 Castles in the sky 42

Altostratus family **44**

Cirrus family **46**

13 Fibrous cirrus 48

14 Mares' tails 50

15 Wave clouds 52

Cirrocumulus family . . **54**

16 Grains-of-rice sky 56

Cirrostratus family . . . **58**

17 Nebulosus and fibrous
cirrostratus 60

18 Mother-of-pearl clouds . . 62

19 Noctilucent clouds 64

Optical phenomena **67**

Rainbows 69

Coronas and rainbow
fringes 71

Ice crystal light shows . . . 73

Haloes 75

Arcs 77

Sun dogs and sun pillars . . 79

Acknowledgements 80

Picture Credits 80

Foreword

Our ever-changing skyscapes are endlessly fascinating. Throughout history, clouds have inspired artists, poets, musicians, and photographers. In most parts of the world, at many times of the year, an array of clouds passes overhead. On calm days, they float gently by, while at other times gales sweep them across the sky at speed. Skyscapes can be calming, dramatic, dull, intriguing, or downright scary. Some have an ethereal beauty that is difficult to describe. Clouds can inform that the weather is likely to remain the same for the foreseeable future, or give clues that change is on its way—for better or for worse.

How you ever wondered how clouds form? Or why some types disappear, only to be replaced by others? Do you ever wish you could put a name to them? Whether your interest is simply in knowing their names, or if you'd like to be able to "read" the sky to forecast tomorrow's weather, this book is for you. It describes the main cloud groups and some of the members that make up each "family". And it explains the conditions responsible for each type. The book also takes a look at some of the fascinating optical phenomena associated with certain clouds.

Tim Harris, London, 2020

(opposite) A massive cumulus congestus coloured by the evening light
(overleaf) A sunset-lit cumulus cloud over the Guatemalan coastline

The nature and naming of clouds

Quite apart from their aesthetic value, human life would not exist were it not for clouds. They make all terrestrial life possible. Clouds are the freshwater delivery mechanism that transports water from the oceans to the land and makes possible the growth of plants and animals.

A cloud is a visible concentration of minute water droplets, ice particles, or a mixture of both, floating in the atmosphere. The vast majority of them are in the lowest layer of the atmosphere, which is called the troposphere. On average, each water droplet has a diameter of about 0.01 mm, but droplets may be much smaller or larger. There are hundreds in each cubic centimetre, millions in every cubic metre. Surface tension keeps them spherical, and currents keep them airborne. Because they are so small, the droplets can remain in liquid form at temperatures as low as –30°C. When still liquid at sub-zero temperatures, they are described as supercooled. At higher levels in the troposphere, clouds are made of ice crystals, which come in many shapes and sizes.

An English amateur meteorologist and artist called Luke Howard named the clouds in the early nineteenth century. He proposed three principle categories—cumulus, stratus, and cirrus—and their modifiers. There have been a few additions, but his names pretty much stuck. When trying to identify a cloud, the key pointers to look for are whether it is heaped (a type of cumulus), flat (a type of stratus), or wispy (a type of cirrus); how low its base is; and whether rain or snow is falling from it. Clouds are named from a combination of their appearance, altitude, and ability to produce precipitation. The names are derived from five Latin words: *Alto* – rain; *Cirrus* – curled; *Cumulus* – heaped; *Nimbus* – rain; *Stratus* – layered. Additionally, *lenticularis* is Latin for lens-shaped; *mammatus* means breast-shaped; and *pyro* means fire.

How clouds form

A parcel of air is a little like a sponge: it can hold water vapour. Warm air can hold more than cool air, but whatever its temperature it can only accommodate so much before it becomes saturated. Then, tiny water droplets condense around even tinier particles of dust or salt and form cloud. One of two things can cause the air to become saturated: either the amount of water vapour in the air parcel increases, or its temperature falls. For example, if air moves over the ocean or a lake, it picks up evaporating water vapour as it goes. Warm air will pick up more than cold air. If this air then rises, for example if it reaches land and passes over a mountain, it will cool. If the cooling continues, the air eventually reaches the point (its dew point) where its water vapour condenses—and cloud develops.

Three primary types of uplift cause cloud to form. Orographic uplift happens when wind pushes air over hills and mountains. Frontal uplift occurs when a wedge of air undercuts another, pushing it higher. Convectional uplift takes place when the ground is heated and causes the air in contact with it to become warmer and rise vertically. Of course, none of these scenarios will produce cloud if the air is bone dry. However, if it is moist, one form of cloud or another will form sooner or later.

The type of cloud that develops depends on whether orographic, frontal, or convective processes are dominant; how much water vapour the air contains; how quickly the air temperature decreases with altitude; and the wind speed.

(opposite) A "tablecloth" of orographic cloud sits on Cape Town's Table Mountain

CUMULUS FAMILY

Characteristics

Cumulus

Abbreviation: Cu

Appearance: Heaped

Cloud-base: From 2,000 ft (600 m)

Cloud-top: Up to 70,000 ft (21,000 m) in the tropics

Cause: Warming of land and convection

Weather: Wide range, from fair to stormy, and from dry to torrential rain

Cumulus clouds are probably the most familiar. The Latin root of the word *cumulus*, meaning 'heap', is a good descriptor of the appearance of these clouds, but they are very variable. They range from the benign, fluffy "cotton wool" clouds—fair-weather cumulus, or cumulus humilis—of a fine summer's day to towering, menacing cumulonimbus clouds, which bring hailstones, thunder, and lightning, and sometimes even spawn tornadoes.

Whatever their scale, all cumulus clouds develop as a result of convection, warm air rising. As it rises, it cools and any water vapour it contains condenses to produce cloud. Depending on local atmospheric conditions, convection may be very limited, producing small clouds, which may later evaporate again. If the warming process continues, bigger clouds will form. In extreme circumstances these may tower to the top of the troposphere, where they flatten out in gleaming white anvils. Such clouds produce storms.

Cumulus and cumulonimbus have relatively low cloud bases, but the suffix "cumulus" is also added to mid- and high-altitude clouds, altocumulus and cirrocumulus respectively.

1

Characteristics

Cumulus humilis
Abbreviation: Cu hum
Appearance:
Shallow and flattish
Cloud-base: 1,000–5,000 ft
(300–1,500 m)
Cause: Warming of
land and convection
Composition:
Water droplets,
sometimes supercooled
Weather: Fine

Fair-weather cumulus

These "cotton-wool" clouds of fair days may be widely spread out or almost touching each other. Often occurring with only light breezes, they have flattish bases, all at the same height. They look mid-grey from beneath although their tops can be dazzlingly white if there are no higher clouds to obscure the Sun.

As with other cumulus clouds, they form where rising air currents caused by a warming land cause water vapour in moist air to condense as tiny water droplets. Fair-weather cumulus does not contain ice crystals. These clouds often form just inland of coastlines, where summer sea breezes carry moist air over warm land. The bottom of the clouds shows the condensation level in the atmosphere. Although fair-weather cumulus clouds never produce rain or snow, they can be the precursors of thicker cloud and rain.

The rising currents within these clouds are generally fairly light. If the air is stable, they remain shallow, sometimes pancake-flat, and may evaporate within a few minutes. However, fair-weather cumulus can also indicate unstable conditions, in which case they are likely to grow bigger and taller—and could develop later into rain-bearing forms of cumulus.

2

Medium cumulus

Characteristics

Cumulus mediocris

Abbreviation: Cu med

Appearance: Gently heaped

Cloud-base: 1,000–5,000 ft
(300–1,500 m)

Cause: Warming of
land and convection,
approach of front

Composition:
Water droplets,
sometimes supercooled

Weather: Generally
dry, but a cold front
could be approaching

While a sky full of fair-weather cumulus has been likened to a flotilla of dinghies, a group of cumulus mediocris is more akin to an armada of galleons. These clouds are at least as tall as they are wide, sometimes with small turrets at the top. Each cloud forms within a column of warm, ascending air, and these currents are quite powerful; inside the cloud, air may rise at more than 17 ft per second (5 m/s). If present in the morning, these clouds indicate atmospheric instability and the likelihood of stormy weather later.

Rows ("cloud streets") of cumulus mediocris can sometimes be seen, lined up in the direction of the prevailing wind. These puffy clouds are often part of a chaotic skyscape with their cumulus cousins—smaller fair-weather cumulus and larger, towering cumulus—and often give warning of the approach of a cold front. In warm or mild conditions, cumulus mediocris produces only very light falls of rain, and this often evaporates before it reaches the ground. Viewed from a distance, these strips of evaporating rain are called virga. In winter, however—if their tops are cold enough—even these relatively small clouds can produce significant falls of snow over the Great Lakes of North America.

3

Towering cumulus

Characteristics

Cumulus congestus
Abbreviation: Cu con
Appearance:
Massively heaped
Cloud-base: 1,000–5,000 ft
(300–1,500 m)
Cloud-top: 20,000 ft
(6,000 m)
Cause: Warming of land,
approach of front
Composition: Mainly
water droplets
Weather: Rain or
snow possible

As their name suggests, towering cumulus clouds are much taller than they are wide and grow into magnificent "cauliflower-topped" shapes. Technically called cumulus congestus, they develop from cumulus mediocris and—in the right conditions—grow into cumulonimbus. Towering cumulus often deliver short, sharp showers. In the tropics, the rain may be torrential—but short-lived. These clouds indicate powerful atmospheric convection and are often a prelude to thunderstorms.

The top of a towering cumulus may be 20,000 ft (6,000 m) above the ground in the tropics, where the tropopause (the boundary between the troposphere and the stratosphere) is at its highest. At this altitude, the cloud's water droplets are supercooled to as cold as -30°C and there may also be ice crystals. Rising currents within the cloud exceed a ferocious 33 ft per second (10 m/s). Rapidly growing towering cumulus may have a veil-like cap, or pileus, made of ice crystals above its highest peak. However, they don't always transform into cumulonimbus—their growth may be suppressed if a layer of higher cloud reduces the Sun's radiation and limits convection. So-called turkey towers are isolated examples that build and collapse in less than an hour.

4

Fire cloud

Characteristics
Cumulus flammagenitus
or pyrocumulus
Abbreviation: Cu flgen
Appearance: Massively
heaped, brown or grey
Cloud-base: 1,000–5,000 ft
(300–1,500 m)
Cloud-top: 30,000 ft
(9,000 m) or more
Cause: Intense
heat from fire
Composition: Water
droplets and smoke
Weather: Heavy rain
and lightning possible

One form of towering cumulus forms under very special conditions: when extreme heat at the surface creates powerful convection currents. This may happen over large forest or bush fires, or over an erupting volcano. The very hot air rises and expands, and water vapour within it condenses once it reaches the air's dew point, forming dense cloud. These pyrocumulus (or cumulus flammagenitus) clouds look dirty yellow-brown or grey because of the ash and smoke they contain, but they are not simply billowing columns of smoke—they are mostly made up of water droplets, as with any other kind of cumulus cloud.

The soot particles generated by the fire are larger than the dust that floats in cleaner air. That means bigger raindrops can condense around them, so torrential rain is possible. The raindrops falling from a cloud that formed over a huge forest fire in the Amazon in 1995 were measured at 0.4 in (1.0 cm) in diameter. A pyrocumulus can help or hinder the fire that created it. On the one hand, heavy rainfall may help extinguish a bush fire. Conversely, really large pyrocumulus, such as that over an erupting volcano, may produce lightning that strikes nearby dry grassland or forest to ignite more fires.

5

Cumulonimbus

Characteristics

Abbreviation: Cb
Appearance:
Massively heaped
Cloud-base: From
2,000 ft (600 m)
Cloud-top: Up to 70,000 ft
(21,000 m) in the tropics
Cause: Fronts,
heating of land
Composition: Water
droplets and ice crystals
Weather: Heavy rain
or hail likely; gusty;
some lightning

The gleaming white mass of a distant cumulonimbus illuminated by bright sunshine is one of the most dramatic cloudscapes there is. This mountainous cloud type develops from cumulus congestus, first as an upward-thrusting cauliflower and finally as a huge "anvil". Cumulonimbus is most common in the tropics and subtropics, and in summer in temperate regions. The biggest cumulonimbus cells may be 60 miles (100 km) or more across. Smaller examples often grow along the line of a cold front.

The dynamics of a cumulonimbus cloud can be likened to an atmospheric engine. To develop, it requires moisture, unstable air, and heat. As warm, moist air rises it cools and water vapour condenses around dust particles in the air. Condensation releases latent heat, which warms the air and accelerates the process of lift and expansion.

As the cloud gets taller, strong updrafts and downdrafts develop. These air currents may exceed 50 ft per second (15 m/s), making them hazardous for aircraft. In the tropics, where the tropopause is highest, the top of the cloud may reach 50,000 ft (15,000 m) or more. The electrical charges that build up between the particles of water and ice eventually produce lightning, which may be persistent. Heavy rain, hail, or—in winter—snow falls.

6

Anvil cloud

Characteristics
Cumulonimbus
capillatus and incus
Abbreviation: Cb cap,
Cb inc
Appearance: Very tall
with broad, flat top
Height: Up to 70,000 ft
(21,000 m)
Cause: Heating of land
Composition: Water
droplets and ice crystals
Weather: Lightning,
strong gusts of wind,
torrential rain or hail

There are several stages in the growth of a cumulonimbus. Before its top flattens out at the tropopause, it is called congestus calvus. Then a veil of wispy cirrus called capillatus ("hair") shrouds the top and as the rising cloud reaches the tropopause it flattens and spreads wide into the characteristic anvil shape of a fully mature cloud, called cumulonimbus incus ("anvil").

It does this because above the tropopause, the air in the stratosphere is much warmer than the air in the cloud, so generally it caps any further ascent. In extreme situations, a dome of cloud may rise above the flat top, where the momentum of the rising air pushes the tropopause higher. The highest tropical cumulonimbus clouds tower to 70,000 ft (21,000 m) and come with the full suite of torrential rain and incessant lightning. The dual problems for aircraft are the violent air currents and the risk of icing as supercooled water droplets freeze to the wings and fuselage.

From beneath, the cloud looks very dark. Downdrafts from the cloud produce strong gusts of wind. If conditions for cloud-building are good, several cumulonimbus may coalesce to form a multi-cell system, which may produce tornadoes.

7

Mammatus

Characteristics

Appearance:
Hanging pouches
Height: 1,100–6,500 ft
(330–2,000 m)
Cause: Downdrafts
in cumulonimbus
Composition: Water
droplets and ice crystals
Weather: Lightning,
strong gusts of wind,
torrential rain or hail,
tornadoes possible

One of the most dramatic—even menacing—clouds, especially if caught by the light of the setting Sun, mammatus often forewarns of extreme weather in the next hour. Lightning, hail, and torrential rain may be imminent. And in the United States, this is tornado weather. Mammatus have also been seen on the underside of volcanic ash clouds. The individual cells of this feature—and there may be hundreds of them—look like pouches or (more rarely) elongated tubes hanging from the base of a cumulonimbus cloud. The pouches may all be of a similar size, or they may be much more variable. They form where cool air is sinking out of the cloud. Mammatus is not a species of cloud in its own right but a feature associated with cumulonimbus, indicating that a powerful storm is very close—or already overhead. A benign form of mammatus can develop under altostratus cloud.

Individual mammatus lobes are short-lived features, typically lasting for about 10 minutes, but a whole cluster may persist for hours under a particularly large cumulonimbus storm cell. They are composed of water droplets, ice crystals, or a mix of the two. Meteorologists do not understand fully how they form.

STRATUS FAMILY

Characteristics

Stratus

Abbreviation: St

**Appearance:
Featureless sheet**

**Cloud-base: Usually
surface–2,000 ft (0–600 m)**

**Cause: Advection, either
associated with high
pressure or approaching
warm front**

**Composition:
Water droplets**

**Weather: Often
overcast, dry or wet**

Stratus is low or very low cloud. It often forms a nondescript pale grey to off-white sheet across the sky and has been described as "tupperware sky". The name stratus means "flattened" in Latin, a reference to this cloud's uniform base. Stratus may form in several ways, when the cloud-base of stratocumulus gets lower, for example. In anticyclonic conditions, when air pressure is high and winds are very light, stratus can persist for days.

Shallow stratus can form after a chilly night when radiation fog has formed in the lowest, coldest valley bottoms. In the morning, as the ground warms, the fog lifts, leaving a shallow sheet of stratus. Observers on high vantage points overlooking the valley will then be treated to spectacular views of the top of the cloud—a beautiful dazzling-white sight as the morning sunshine illuminates it.

If stratus clouds produce any precipitation—and usually they don't—generally it will only be drizzle, fine rain, or snow grains. One exception is darker, thicker nimbostratus, which often attends the passage of a warm front. This can produce miserable, gloomy conditions with persistent rain. When it is raining, the cloud-base of nimbostratus is often completely indistinguishable.

8

Featureless stratus

Characteristics
Stratus nebulosus
Abbreviation:
St neb and St fra
Appearance: Featureless
sheet, continuous
or broken
Cloud-base: Usually
surface–2,000 ft (0–600 m)
Cause: Moist air passing
over cool land or sea
Composition:
Water droplets
Weather: Usually
dull, dry, and calm

Featureless stratus (stratus nebulosus) is arguably the dullest of all clouds. Think of a calm autumn or winter day, with high pressure dominating and the Sun being hidden for hours on end—yet it doesn't rain. The cloud-base ranges from ground level—when it is fog—to 2,000 ft (600 m) or more, but it is hard to see exactly where the cloud begins because it is so nebulous. Despite its gloominess, this form of stratus rarely produces much precipitation, but "scotch mist", drizzle, or very light snow (in winter) are possible. The densest form of stratus is completely opaque, obliterating the Sun, while a shallower version makes the Sun appear as a fairly bright disc. The transition from one to the other is often a sign that the cloud sheet is dissipating and finer weather is on its way.

Stratus often forms in calm, anticyclonic conditions when moist air passes from relatively mild sea to move over cooler land—or vice versa. If the wind picks up, the blanket of stratus will start to break up, forming ragged scuds of low cloud that lack the "cotton wool" character of fair-weather cumulus. This is cumulus fractus, which also forms when stratus moves over warmer land or sea and begins to fragment. This is a sign of improving weather.

9

Nimbostratus

Characteristics

Nimbostratus

Abbreviation: Ns

Appearance: Continuous featureless sheet

Cloud-base: Usually surface–9,000 ft (0–2,750 m)

Cause: Approaching front

Composition: Water droplets

Weather: Persistent rain or snow

The archetypal rain cloud, nimbostratus is featureless, thick, grey cloud from which rain or snow often falls steadily—maybe for hours without a break. In temperate latitudes, 1 in (2.5 cm) or more of rain may fall in a day at low altitudes, while in hills the figure may be much higher. Nimbostratus clouds deposit huge volumes of water on South Asia during the monsoon season—up to 12 in (30 cm) on the wettest days.

This multi-layer cloud is usually 6,500–13,000 ft (2,000–4,000 m) thick—enough to blot out sunshine completely, and its base is not clearly defined. Ragged clumps of clouds called pannus may form below its base.

Most common at mid-latitudes, nimbostratus usually develops as sheets of medium-level altostratus get thicker in advance of a warm front. This cloud may persist for hours or days, depending on the speed of the front it precedes. Slowly rising warm air along the front produces sheets of clouds at all levels. High-altitude cirrostratus appears first, then mid-level altostratus, and finally nimbostratus. Unlike cumulonimbus clouds, it does not produce lightning, but occasionally where convection is particularly vigorous along a warm front, cumulonimbus may form within thick blankets of nimbostratus.

ALTOCUMULUS FAMILY

Characteristics
Altocumulus
Abbreviation: Ac
Appearance:
Small clumps
Cloud-base: 6,500–18,000 ft
(2,000–5,000 m)
Cause: Break-up of
altostratus; warm rising
air; atmospheric waves
in lee of mountains
Composition: Water
droplets or ice crystals
Weather: Fair and dry, but
often a precursor of rain

This family is made up of mid-altitude clouds. They come in a variety of shapes and sizes, but typically a patch of altocumulus is made up of clumps or rolls of cloud. The individual elements, or cloudlets, are usually close together and appear smaller than those of stratocumulus but larger than those of higher-altitude cirrocumulus. Although altocumulus is usually seen in fair weather, it often precedes the arrival of lower, thicker cloud and rain (nimbostratus) as a warm front moves closer.

Unlike cirrocumulus, the underside of altocumulus shows some grey shading. These clouds are mostly supercooled water droplets but there may also be ice crystals. They don't often produce precipitation, but when they do, it usually rather appears as wispy virga hanging beneath the cloud than reaching the ground.

The most common type of altocumulus is flattish and is called stratiformis, or "mackerel sky". There may be two layers, one above the other, and it sometimes forms when a sheet of altostratus begins to break up. Other members of the family include tufty floccus, turret-shaped castellanus, and lens-shaped lenticularis. Several of these may be present in a single chaotic skyscape, along with nimbostratus and higher-level clouds.

10

Characteristics

Altocumulus stratiformis

Abbreviation: Ac str

Appearance: Small clumps close together, sometimes filling much of the sky

Cloud-base: 6,500–18,000 ft (2,000–5,500 m)

Cause: Convection, or break-up of altostratus

Composition: Water droplets or ice crystals

Weather: Fair and dry, either a precursor of rain or when rain has recently passed

Mackerel sky

Mackerel skies can form with mid-level altocumulus or with higher cirrocumulus. Altocumulus stratiformis is the most common form of altocumulus and can be seen in most parts of the world. Although this white or pale grey cloud is made up of many small components, it is flattish, with very little vertical extent. Altocumulus, which is generally made up of water droplets, sometimes covers most of the sky. The thinnest, almost transparent form perlucidus may be only 300 ft (90 m) thick.

One piece of weather lore associated with this cloud is "*Mackerel sky, mackerel sky. Never long wet and never long dry*". This warns that a combination of the appearance of altocumulus clouds and falling air pressure signals that the weather won't be dry for much longer. Rain is likely within 6–12 hours, though it won't persist for long. And conversely, the presence of this cloud with rising barometric pressure indicates that a frontal system has already passed, ushering in a period of better weather.

Altocumulus arranged in long, parallel lines, either merged or completely separate, is called undulatus. These very photogenic clouds are reminiscent of ripples of water.

11

Lens and pancake clouds

Characteristics

Altocumulus lenticularis
Abbreviation: Ac len
Appearance: Lens-shaped,
sometimes stacked
Cloud-base: 6,500–16,500 ft
(2,000–5,000 m)
Cause: Convection, or
break-up of altostratus
Composition: Water
droplets or ice crystals
Weather: Fair and
dry, either a precursor
of rain or when rain
has recently passed

Some of the most beautiful clouds form downwind of mountains and hills in fine weather. These lens-shaped (lenticular) clouds have smooth, well-defined outlines. When wind encounters a physical barrier, such as a mountain, orographic lift carries the air over the summit and may form one or more standing waves on the far side. These are called lee waves. If the air is moist and the crest of the wave is above the lifted condensation level (above which water vapour condenses to form cloud), a lens cloud forms.

Although air continuously passes through the wave—at 35 mph (55 km/h) or more—the cloud remains stationary. Lee waves form even when the air is very dry—they just don't produce clouds. The height of the cloud-base is related to the dew point and the height of the mountain barrier. Skilled glider pilots know that air is rising at the leading edge of a lenticular cloud and falling at the trailing edge so they may make for the former to gain "wave lift". Very high-altitude lenticular clouds are called cirrocumulus lenticularis.

Sometimes there is not just one lens cloud but a whole pile of them, one on top of another. They can look like a stack of plates. The most spectacular of these have a series of lenses that are separated from each other, like a series of floating discs. These "pancake clouds" occur when the atmosphere's relative humidity varies with height. If moist and dry layers alternate, cloud will form in the moist "strata" but not the dry. The result is a set of stacked clouds, which imaginative observers have mistaken for UFOs in poor light.

The best places to look for lens and pancake clouds is downwind of any range of high hills or mountains. In the UK, the Yorkshire side of the Pennines and areas to the east of the Cambrian, Cairngorm, or Grampian Mountains are good places to look when the prevailing wind is from the west or south-west. In North America, they can be seen downwind of many peaks in the Rockies. Some of the most spectacular form in the "Sierra Wave", which occurs when westerly winds blow over California's Sierra Nevada Range.

12

Characteristics

Altocumulus castellanus
Abbreviation: Ac cas
Appearance: "Fairy
castle" turrets
Cloud-base: 6,500–20,000 ft
(2,000–6,000 m)
Cause: Convection
at mid-altitudes
in troposphere
Composition: Water
droplets or ice crystals
Weather: Fine, but a
thunderstorm may
be imminent

Castles in the sky

If the sky has billowing clouds, reminiscent of the turrets of a castle but with their bases thousands of feet higher than cumulus clouds, a thunderstorm may not be far away. These towering altocumulus castellanus give clues to what is happening in the mid-troposphere.

Air temperature usually falls with greater altitude. The rate at which this happens is called the lapse rate. If, thousands of feet up, there's a layer of air whose temperature is falling more quickly with height, this produces something called mid-altitude instability. This means that if a parcel of warm, moist air rises as far as this boundary its water vapour will condense—and it will then rise more rapidly, forming towers of cloud. These are much smaller than a towering cumulus or cumulonimbus, but pilots nevertheless try to avoid them because the air around them is turbulent.

Large raindrops may fall from castellanus clouds although they usually evaporate before they reach the ground. If the unstable conditions continue, the towers will grow together into a much larger cumulonimbus. Then, torrential rain and lightning is likely.

ALTOSTRATUS FAMILY

Characteristics

Altostratus

Abbreviation: As

Appearance: Featureless or slightly undulating sheet, with Sun usually visible

Cloud-base: 6,500–23,000 ft (2,000–7,000 m)

Cause: Gently rising air in advance of warm front or behind a cold front

Composition: Water droplets or ice crystals

Weather: Dry, but if cloud is thickening, a precursor of rain

A sheet of greyish-white cloud at medium elevation is likely to be altostratus. It is paler than nimbostratus but darker than cirrostratus. It may be only 3,300 ft (1,000 m) thick, in which case the disc of the Sun will be weakly visible through it. In the tropics, it can be as deep as 16,500 ft (5,000 m), however. Unlike cirrostratus, altostratus prevents objects on the ground from casting shadows, and it does not usually produce a halo around the Sun or Moon.

Light rain or snow may fall from altostratus. This appears as virga "hanging" from the base of the cloud but it doesn't reach the ground. If the cloud thickens and the sky gets darker, the altostratus will probably be replaced by rain-bearing nimbostratus in advance of a warm front. But it may also appear after the passage of a cold front, in which case it is likely to usher in a period of fair weather.

A red-hued sheet of altocumulus seen in the western sky at sunset prompts the old saying *"Red sky at night, shepherd's delight"*. A red sky appears when dust is trapped in the atmosphere by the sinking air of a ridge of high air pressure. The dust scatters blue light, leaving red light to give the sky its distinctive appearance. A red sky at sunset means high pressure is advancing from the west, promising a dry, sunny tomorrow.

CIRRUS FAMILY

Characteristics
Cirrus
Abbreviation: Ci
Appearance: Wisps, very
small clumps, or sheets
Cloud-base:
16,500–60,000 ft
(5,000–18,000 m)
Cause: Gentle convection
of dryish air; remains
of aircraft contrails
Composition: Ice crystals
Weather: Fair and dry

The name cirrus comes from the Latin word *cirr*, a curl of hair. All the clouds in the cirrus family form at very high elevations. The most familiar are the hooked, wispy shapes of "mares' tail" cirrus, and other forms include streaks aligned with the wind direction, denser patches that were once the tops of decayed cumulonimbus, extensive sheets of cirrostratus, and the fine dappling of cirrocumulus. Cirrus can develop from contrails, the water vapour from the exhaust of aircraft jet engines.

Based on satellite data, the various forms of cirrus cover 20–25 percent of the Earth's surface at any one time, that figure rising to 70 percent in the tropics—but it is often unseen from the ground because it is obscured by lower clouds.

All cirrus clouds are made from fine ice crystals. Whereas at lower elevations water condenses to form water droplets, at heights above 18,000 ft/5,500 m (21,000 ft/6,500 m in the tropics), the small quantity of water vapour in dry air can change directly to ice, a process called *deposition*. The crystals average 0.01 in long, but some are much smaller. Since the atmosphere is relatively dry at these altitudes, cirrus clouds are generally very shallow.

When sunlight passes through ice clouds it may be refracted, and this accounts for optical phenomena associated with cirriform clouds, such as sun dogs and haloes around the Sun and Moon.

13

Fibrous cirrus

Characteristics

Cirrus fibratus
Abbreviation: Ci fib
Appearance: White
parallel streaks
Cloud-base:
20,000–60,000 ft
(6,000–18,000 m)
Cause: Gentle convection
of dryish air
Composition: Ice crystals
Weather: Fair and dry

Looking like someone has drawn a comb across the sky, fibrous cirrus is made up of hundreds or thousands of bright white parallel streaks. They may be straight or slightly curving but they lack the hooked ends of uncinus, or mares' tails. The streaks of fibrous cirrus often run in the same direction as the high-altitude wind, which is often not the same direction as the prevailing wind at ground level.

Since this high-elevation cloud is composed of ice crystals, a halo may form around the Sun when its light is refracted as it passes through the cloud. Fibrous cirrus is often one member of a collection of different cirrus clouds in a chaotic sky. Other types include mares' tails, ragged patches of cirrus floccus, which is reminiscent of cotton wool, and cirrus castellanus, which is taller than it is wide.

All these clouds may give an early warning of thicker, lower cloud moving in during the next day—or they may just be the remnants of an old front that has broken down. In the latter scenario, there's every chance the weather will stay fair.

14

Characteristics

Cirrus uncinus
Abbreviation: Ci unc
Appearance:
Hooked wisps
Cloud-base:
23,000–60,000 ft
(7,000–18,000 m)
Cause: Gentle convection
of dryish air
Composition: Ice crystals
Weather: Fair and dry

Mares' tails

A sky full of mares' tails makes for a spectacular sight, almost as if an artist has taken a brush and some brilliant white paint to the sky. Often associated with fine summer days, they can occur in any season and are sometimes heralds of a change in the weather. Arguably they are even more spectacular at dusk when coloured orange and red by the setting Sun. The technical name for mares' tails is cirrus uncinus. They often share the sky with fibrous cirrus and cirrocumulus.

The word *uncinus* comes from the Latin for hook, and for good reason. These clouds' individual elements differ from fibrous cirrus in having hooked ends. These "hooks" are created by wind shear—the change in wind speed and/or direction with altitude. If the mares' tails thicken, maybe to be replaced with cirrostratus and lower cloud, they herald the approach of a weather front. However, sometimes they are just collections of billions of ice crystals spreading out from a dying cumulonimbus cloud. Like other cirrus clouds, mares' tails are composed of ice crystals and form at heights where the air is colder than -40°C.

15 Wave clouds

Characteristics

No abbreviation
adopted by World
Meteorological Organization
Appearance: Repeated
breaking-wave pattern
Cloud-base:
16,500–40,000 ft
(5,000–12,000 m)
Cause: Wind shear
Composition: Water
droplets or ice crystals
Weather: Breezy but dry

Wave, or fluctus, clouds are memorable—but usually very short-lived. They look bizarrely like breaking waves in the sky, with the wave crests curled over. Also called Kelvin–Helmholtz (K–H) clouds, they are unusual because they only occur when there is a particular combination of circumstances.

These clouds depend on something called wind shear. This happens at the boundary of two different masses of air, one sitting above the other, when the wind above is blowing faster than the air below. The boundary between the two layers becomes uneven and turbulent. If the air is too dry for cloud to form, the boundary is invisible. But aircraft pilots know that K–H turbulence gives rise to bumpy flight conditions—better known as clear-air turbulence.

However, if the air is damp enough, cloud forms at the boundary and its top surface is blown into the surreal shapes characteristic of a fluctus cloud. Sometimes, these clouds form with altocumulus or stratus, but the most dramatic examples are much higher. Incidentally, K–H turbulence is also responsible for the "white horses" that form on the ocean on windy days.

CIRROCUMULUS FAMILY

Characteristics
Cirrocumulus
Abbreviation: Cc
Appearance: Tiny
white cloudlets
Cloud-base:
18,000–49,000 ft
(5,500–15,000 m)
Cause: Gentle convection
of dryish air
Composition: Mostly
ice crystals
Weather: Fair and dry

Some of the most delicate, beautiful skyscapes feature hundreds or thousands of tiny cloudlets arranged in regular patterns at great height. These are cirrocumulus clouds, the higher-altitude version of mackerel sky, so named because they look like the scaly skin of a fish. Around sunset, when they take on yellow, orange, or red hues, they are truly spectacular. They are thin, transparent, and have an almost ethereal quality.

Cirrocumulus clouds are made of ice crystals and supercooled water droplets. They grow when air containing moisture rises gently in the upper troposphere, or when an extensive sheet of cirrostratus is breaking up. Although some snow may fall from cirrocumulus, it evaporates long before it reaches the ground.

Cirrocumulus may be swept across the sky at 100 mph (160 km/h) or more by super-fast high-level winds. If its cover increases steadily from one direction, this means thicker, lower cloud is on its way as a frontal system approaches. Strong winds and rain may be 18 hours away, or less. Hence the old warning to the crews of sailing ships, "*Mackerel sky and mares' tails make tall ships carry low sails*". Mariners lowered their sails in advance of damaging gales.

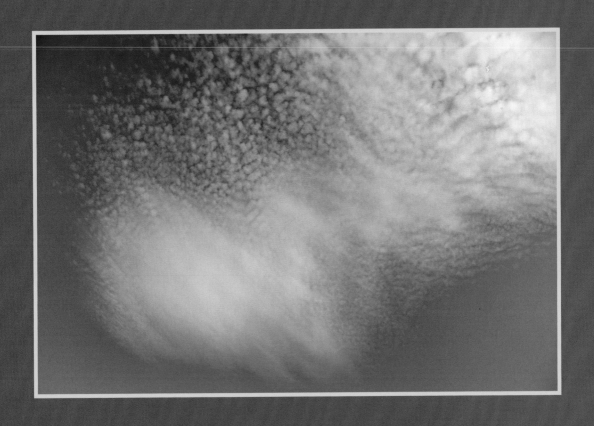

16

Grains-of-rice sky

Characteristics

Cirrocumulus stratiformis
Abbreviation:
Cc str, Cc un, Cc cas
Appearance: Tiny
white cloudlets
Cloud-base:
18,000–49,000 ft
(5,500–15,000 m)
Cause: Gentle convection,
movement of one air
mass past another
Composition: Ice crystals
Weather: Fair and dry

Different types of cirrocumulus give clues to their origin and what the weather is likely to do next. Extensive sheets of hundreds or thousands of cirrocumulus cloudlets, reminiscent of grains of rice, have the technical name stratiformis. Alternatively, if the tiny elements of cloud are arranged in rows or billows with clear, parallel gaps between them, the cloud is known as undulatus. This forms when a body of moist, slightly warmer air pushes past dry, colder air, forming ripples like those formed as a current of water flows over sand. The ripples run at right angles to the direction of the high-altitude wind.

If the cirrocumulus cloudlets are taller than they are wide, that tells us that vigorous convection is taking place at a great height, with warm air rising into a colder layer above. These are cirrocumulus castellanus clouds and they forewarn that a giant cumulonimbus cloud may not be far away—bringing thunder, lightning, heavy rain, and hail.

Fallstreak holes, or "hole-punch clouds", have been mistaken for UFOs. They occasionally develop in special circumstances when an aircraft flies through a cirrocumulus sky, forming an expanding rounded hole.

CIRROSTRATUS FAMILY

Notable for the often-spectacular optical phenomena it produces, cirrostratus is a transparent, generally featureless cloud of the upper troposphere. Like other very high-altitude clouds, it is made of tiny ice crystals. It is the very best for looking for haloes, sun dogs, and sun pillars. In fact, sometimes the presence of a halo around the Sun may be the only indication that there is any cloud in the sky, so thin can a layer of cirrostratus be. These features are most likely when the cloud's veil is very thin; if it thickens, they fade.

The traditional saying, "*When halo rings Moon or Sun, rain's approaching on the run*" refers to this cloud's value in forecasting a deterioration in the weather. Although, just like cirrus and cirrocumulus, cirrostratus doesn't produce rain or snow at the ground, if it begins to thicken then persistent rain is likely within 8–24 hours. To confirm this, watch for the appearance of altocumulus. Superficially, cirrocumulus and thin altocumulus can look the same. A good way to differentiate them is to apply the shadow test: if the Sun casts a shadow, it is shining through cirrocumulus; if there's not shadow, the cloud is altocumulus.

Not all cirrocumulus informs of rain on the way. Small patches, often with cirrus and cirrocumulus nearby, may indicate the last remnants of a weather front that is no longer active.

17

Nebulosus and fibrous cirrostratus

Characteristics

Abbreviation:
Cs neb, Cs dup, Cs fib
Appearance: Transparent
veil, either featureless
or fibrous
Cloud-base:
16,500–43,000 ft
(5,000–13,000 m)
Cause: Gentle convection,
movement of one air
mass past another
Composition: Ice crystals
Weather: Fair and dry

The most common form of cirrostratus is the uniform, featureless nebulosus. This is translucent, sometimes to the point of invisibility. Thicker sheets cause sunshine to appear "milky". A sheet of nebulosus may extend for hundreds of miles. But what this cloud lacks in terms of aesthetic appeal is more than made up for by the range of light features produced as sunlight is refracted by its billions of ice crystals. The most common of these is the 22° halo, a circle of light centred on the Sun.

Close observation through binoculars (never close to the Sun!) may show a higher level of cloud visible through breaks in the cirrostratus. This shows that the cloud is multi-layered duplicatus, a species of cirrostratus that has as many as a dozen layers, each only a few hundred feet thick, separated by clear air. Because wind direction often changes with altitude, the layers may not all be moving in exactly the same direction or at the same speed.

If the ice crystals are large enough to fall from the cloud, they will give its underside a fibrous texture more akin to densely packed cirrus. This form of cirrostratus is called fibrosus. The falling crystals evaporate before they fall far below the cloud.

18

Mother-of-pearl clouds

Characteristics

Abbreviation: PSC
Appearance: Iridescent
sheets or lenses
Height: 65,500–100,000 ft
(20,000–30,500 m)
Cause: Fall of temperature
in lower stratosphere
Composition: Very
small ice crystals
Weather: Very
cold and dry

Occasionally seen during very cold and dry conditions in winter, sheets or lenses of mother-of-pearl cloud make for one of the most spectacular sights in the night sky. They are also called nacreous clouds, "nacre" being another word for mother of pearl, the shiny, iridescent layer on the inside of oyster shells. Their technical name is ice polar stratospheric clouds because they form at very high altitudes over polar regions in winter when temperatures in the lower stratosphere fall to -85°C.

Mother-of-pearl clouds are visible only when lit by the Sun's rays when it is 1–6° below the horizon—a little after sunset or before sunrise. Their vivid rainbow iridescence can be explained by the small size of the ice crystals from which they are made. These scatter the Sun's light differently from those in lower, less cold clouds. Although rare, mother-of-pearl clouds are best looked for on otherwise clear winter nights over Scotland, Scandinavia, Russia, Alaska, Canada, and Antarctica.

Although few other clouds are likely to be present at the same time, there may be some high, wispy cirrus. After sunset, this will turn grey and appear as shadows against the even higher mother-of-pearl clouds, which will still be glowing brightly.

19

Noctilucent clouds

Characteristics

Abbreviation: NLC

Appearance: Bluish-white
sheet, streaks, or billows

Height: 280,000–300,000 ft
(8,500–9,000 m)

Cause: Unknown

Composition: Tiny
ice crystals

Weather: Clear and dry

Unlike mother-of-pearl clouds, noctilucent ("illuminated at night") clouds are most likely to be seen in summer—shortly after sunset or shortly before dawn. While not as colourful as mother-of-pearl clouds, they are no less dramatic as they illuminate then dim again in the evening or early morning sky. Brightest when the Sun is about 10° below the horizon, they first appear pale blue, then brighter bluish-white and vivid electric-blue, before fading again.

These clouds form at phenomenal heights—around 280,000–300,000 ft (85,000–90,000 m)—in the mesosphere, which is the third layer of the Earth's atmosphere. They develop only when temperatures fall below -120° C, something that only happens in summer at this height. Noctilucent clouds take many forms: sheets, streaks, billows, or whirls. They are made up of ultra-fine ice crystals, which probably form on nuclei of cosmic dust from micro-meteors.

Noctilucent clouds are most likely to be seen from mid-May to mid-August at latitudes between 50° and 70°. They don't form nearer to the equator, and at higher latitudes there isn't enough summer darkness for them to be visible.

OPTICAL PHENOMENA

When the white light of the Sun's rays passes through water droplets or the ice crystals in clouds, it may be refracted—bent and split into its component colours. This can also happen when moonlight passes through clouds. However, conditions have to be just right for this to happen. For a start, the light has to be able to pass through the cloud, and this only happens with thin varieties, mostly cirrus, cirrostratus, and thin altostratus and altocumulus. Thicker clouds such as cumulus and stratus reflect sunlight back into space.

Some of these light displays are produced as the Sun's rays shine on or through water droplets in rain or cloud, while others result from the passage of light through ice crystals in high, cold clouds. The most beautiful of them all, and the most frequently seen, is simply the product of sunlight shining onto raindrops—the rainbow.

One word of warning, though. Staring at the Sun is dangerous and can result in damage to the retinas of the eyes. So be careful when looking for, or at, any clouds or optical phenomena close to it. Never look at the Sun itself, even for a second, but hide it behind the edge of a building or a post when viewing. And if photographing near the Sun, make sure to use a solar filter.

(opposite) A 22° halo rings the Sun and a vertical sun pillar links the two

Rainbows

The magical, colourful arc of a rainbow appears because of the physical qualities of light and raindrops. When the white light of the Sun's rays passes into a raindrop, they are refracted—bent and split into their component colours—then some are reflected out again. Red and orange light is not bent as much as violet and indigo light, so a rainbow appears as a series of concentric bands of colour. The sequence, from the outside of the arc in, is red, orange, yellow, green, blue, indigo, violet, which I like to remember with the aid of the silly mnemonic *"Rinse Out Your Granny's Boots In Vinegar"*.

A number of conditions must apply in order for a rainbow to appear. Rain must be falling, and the Sun has to be shining behind the observer and relatively low in the sky (at an elevation of 42° or less). In fact, the lower the Sun, the greater the rainbow's arc; a full 180° semicircle can only be seen when the Sun is actually on the horizon at dawn or dusk. If a double rainbow is visible, the outer of the two parallel arcs is paler and its colour sequence is reversed.

Rainbows are only seen where cloud cover is broken—after all, the Sun needs to be shining—so this is a phenomenon associated with cumulonimbus downpours or towering cumulus showers rather than horizon-to-horizon nimbostratus.

(opposite) A rainbow forms an arch over a forested valley

Coronas and rainbow fringes

Coronas form when light is diffracted by water droplets. Although superficially similar, they are not formed in the same way as haloes, which are produced by ice crystals in high clouds. Coronas are more likely to be seen around the Sun or Moon when it is partly obscured by lower clouds. The most common form of corona appears at night when the Moon sits behind a patch of altostratus and the lunar light is diffracted into its rainbow constituents. The smaller the cloud's water droplets, the larger the corona.

When parts of a cloud are thin and made of similar-sized water droplets, their fringes sometimes shine with pastel hues of red, orange, yellow, green, and mauve. This iridescence is often seen in lenticular altocumulus clouds, because their droplets have a similar history and are likely to be the same size. Since this phenomenon usually occurs close to the Sun, extra care has to be taken when viewing it. Make sure the Sun itself is hidden or—better still—view the cloud's reflection in water.

(opposite) Iridescence around the margins of a lenticular cloud

Ice crystal light shows

Ice crystals are responsible for most of the amazing light shows in the troposphere. The crystals form hexagonal prisms, and although these vary in proportion and shape, they have identical angles between their faces. It is this consistency that produces predictable shapes in the sky—haloes, arcs, and columns of light. In the most incredible displays, the whole sky can become webbed by intricate arcs.

Most ice crystals are hexagonal plates or columns, but some are pyramidal. It is the combination of crystals' size and shape, and their alignment relative to sunlight or moonlight, that determines what kind of optical phenomena—if any—they produce. Plate crystals tend to align like falling leaves, with their flat faces almost horizontal. They produce many kinds of haloes that encircle the Sun or Moon. Columnar crystals often line up with the long axis horizontal, and these are responsible for a variety of arcs and parhelia, features that curve away from the Sun. Pyramidal crystals produce what are known as odd radius haloes, at 9°, 18°, 20°, 23°, 24°, and 35°.

(opposite) A rare combination of a 22° halo, sun dogs to the left and right of the Sun, and an upper tangential arc in winter cirrostratus

Haloes

Haloes, or ice bows, are circles of white light centred on the Sun or Moon. Most often seen when cirrostratus covers the sky, they come in several sizes. The saying "*Ring around the Moon means rain soon*", is based on the pretty astute observation that this halo-producing cloud is often a precursor of a frontal system.

The most common halo, with a radius of 22°, was found by researchers in Germany to occur on about 100 days each year. This halo shows a red fringe on the inside and—more rarely—other colours of the rainbow arranged concentrically around it. Its radius can easily be verified by standing with your arm stretched and fingers spread. Given that the span between little finger and thumb is roughly 20°, with your thumb placed in front of the Sun, the halo should be at the tip of your little finger.

Haloes come in other sizes, too. Small 9° models are seen less frequently than the 22° variety, and 46° haloes are fainter than their cousins. They show red, orange, and yellow, but no greens or blues. The very fortunate sky-watcher may see a series of concentric haloes, with bright sun dogs either side of the real Sun on the middle ring. This amazing spectacle is most likely to be seen at high latitudes when the Sun is low in the sky and veiled with cirrostratus.

(opposite) The 22° halo is the most commonly seen variety, here created by fibrous cirrus

Arcs

Circumzenithal arcs are seen less frequently than haloes, but they are no less spectacular. This feature forms if a thin covering of cirrostratus or cirrus lies in front of the Sun, which must be low in the sky. Additionally, the cloud's plate-shaped ice crystals must be drifting pretty much horizontally. This arc looks like an upside-down rainbow, with the red on the underside, and has been described as a "smile in the sky". Its lowest point always lies directly over the Sun. Sometimes seen in the company of a pair of sun dogs, a circumzenithal arc very rarely forms a full circle (which is known as a Kern arc), in which case the red is on the outside.

Unlike a circumzenithal arc, upper and lower tangent arcs touch a 22° halo immediately above and below the Sun. The upper arc has a gull-winged profile whose "wings" droop as the Sun rises higher in the sky. Tangent arcs are produced when sunlight passes through hexagonal column-shaped ice crystals. A saucer-shaped parhelic circle passes through the Sun and the sun dogs either side. This unusual phenomenon appears when the cirrostratus is a mixture of correctly aligned plate and column crystals.

(opposite) An upper tangent arc lies tangential to a halo and there are sun dogs to the left and right of the Sun

Sun dogs and sun pillars

Sun dogs, mock suns, or parhelia are sometimes seen when a sheet of cirrostratus veils the Sun when it is low in the sky. They form a pair of bright white lights about 22° to the left and right of it and at the same elevation. Although not common, sun dogs are most likely in middle latitudes in winter, often in association with haloes. Sun dogs may show at least some rainbow colours, with red on the side nearest the Sun and violet on the outside. Like other optical phenomena, they appear when sunlight is refracted as it passes through millions of ice crystals in high clouds.

Sun pillars are best looked for around dawn and dusk when the Sun's rays pass through cirrostratus or relatively thick cirrus. They are narrow beams of light extending vertically above and below the Sun, and they often take on the yellow, orange, or red hues of sunrise or sunset. At high latitudes, a pillar seen at sunset may follow the Sun north (south in the Southern Hemisphere) for half an hour after it has sunk below the horizon. A sun pillar appears above the Sun when its rays are reflected downwards from the underside of plate-shaped ice crystals in cirrostratus or cirrus clouds. If extending below the Sun light is reflected from the upper side of these crystals. Sun pillars are more commonly seen from aircraft.

(opposite) Although the dawn Sun has not risen above the horizon, its light reflects from cirrostratus ice crystals to form a bright orange pillar

Acknowledgements

The author would like to thank his brother Bob for commenting on the text and making suggestions regarding convection in the upper troposphere.

Picture Credits

All photos from Shutterstock.

LeManna (front cover); Lukas Jonaitis (pp. 2–3); dlamb302 (p. 6); Byron Ortiz (p. 8); Nathan Chor (p. 10); alybaba (p. 13); kato08 (p. 29); Ioan Panaite (p. 35); katatonia82 (p. 41); Jakpanee Suwannasri (p. 45); Alybaba (p. 47); Sonja Filitz (p. 55); Andrzej Sliwinski (p. 59); Francesco Dazzi (p. 66); Artem Avetisyan (p. 68); Menno van der Haven (p. 70); Arseniy Shemyakin Photo (p. 72); Menno van der Haven (p. 74); Ripitya (p. 76); Martins Vanags (p.78).

Plates: Agness.photography (1); Yes058 (2); Klaus Wagenhaeuser (3); Eugene R Thieszen (4); Allycreations (5); Lamax (6); Menno van der Haven (7); Anna Ilukhina (8); Pharaoh Osiris (9); imageBROKER.com (10); Guido Suard (11); Golubov.Ivana (12); Edgloris Marys (13); Martchan (14); Wayne Broussard (15); Manfred Ruckszio (16); INDz (17); M. Barratt (18); Anna Anikina (19).